AGONY, WHERE IS YOUR STING?

A newfound hope in pain

Jamillah London

AGONY, WHERE IS YOUR STING?
Copyright © 2018 Jamillah London
2nd Edition
2nd Edition edits by Ana White
Publishing by Kendra Sikes for BB Publishing

All rights reserved. No part of this book may be reproduced or transmitted in any form or by any means without written permission from the author. The only exception is the use of short excerpts utilized by a reviewer providing synopsis or review of the text itself.

This text is geared to providing factual and reliable information regarding the topics and issued covered by the author. Trademarks, brands, and landmarks within this book are for clarifying purposes and to advance the narrative of the accounts discussed within the book. The owners themselves maintain direct affiliation and ownership of their product, services, etc. The writer makes no claim of ownership to any mentioned landmark, company, product or service.

Dedication

This book is dedicated to my two beautiful daughters, granddaughters, and my handsome son who lives on in spirit. I also dedicate this book to my mother and grandmother who will always be in my heart until we meet again. To my Aunt Betty, who raised me to become the woman I am today. TO my five siblings, and all family and friends who believed in me. To my publisher Kendra Sikes who helped push me along the way in order to get my book done in a timely manner and encouraged me when I felt like giving up and no longer writing. Lastly, I dedicate this book to my city that showed me a lot of love along the way.

I hope this book encourages someone that feels hopeless and silent. Everyone has a story to tell. Stay strong and encouraged.

In Remembrance

This book honors and is in remembrance of the following:
- My beloved son, Anthony Lorenzo Ramsey, Jr.
- My mother Mary Louise London
- My father Charles Henry London, who passed away in prison after a heart attack
- My grandmother Minnie Allison
- My uncle John Lee Allison
- My Aunt Pat Williams
- "Mousey" Johnny Black
- Ronald Tilgman
- DJ Ronald Jones
- My boyfriend Melvin "Mel" from New York

Table of Contents

(Note: Reference books should always have a Table of Contents, but novels do not require one. If you don't want a Table of Contents, simply delete this entire page.)

Introduction 5
Chapter 1: Friday, April 30.1982 6
Chapter 2: Now What? 11
Chapter 3: This Can't Be Happening!...................... 14
Chapter 4: God, Please Make This Go Away!......... 17
Chapter 5: I'm not Built For This Anymore 21
Chapter 6: The Shift 25
Chapter 7: The Stronghold 27
Chapter 8: A Time For Change 29
Chapter 9: Anthony 32
Chapter 10: The Secret Storm 36
2nd Edition Notes: Handling the Storm 38

Introduction

The key to finding peace in life is something some people never find. You may have it for a moment or for nine years of your life in the form of a mother's love. That peace is something that most people have experienced at some point in their lives. I held that peace, only to have it shattered by the death of my mother, who died at the hands of the only person who should have provided a feeling of security, support, love and peace- My father. My father killed my mother and peace eluded me for decades at a time.

I became a mother and was able to give my son the peace I still had not mastered. Until one day, when that peace would similarly be shattered by his death. The death of my son, my only son, left me speechless. No words can describe the feeling. Although the feelings may subside, they never totally fade away to give you peace. Because of that, my story continues, as does my journey for peace.

I wrote the first edition to find that peace through telling my story. In this second edition, I conclude the book with some lessons that I have learned since writing and publishing the first edition. I am hopeful that it will help those searching for peace, to both relate to my pain and journey, but to also see that peace and lessons were obtainable in that process and aftermath.

Chapter One
Friday, April 30, 1982

I awoke from my bed so excited that it was Friday, the last day of the week for school. I was always used to my oldest sister Charlene getting me dressed for school. Her job was to take care of me and my younger brother Charles. My older sister Estelle had to take care of my other two siblings, Louie and Tamir. We were known as the 'Brady Bunch'.

My mother taught us how to be independent at an early age. She did that intentionally. I decided to dress myself and I always felt great about that. My mother would leave my sisters in charge for the most part because she worked and attended school. She never seemed to have time left for herself. The only time she had was on the weekends, and even then, she would plan either a movies trip or skating as a way to spend time with us.

That day, I got dressed and headed to pick up my neighborhood friend Angie. The day was beautiful, and you could hear the birds chirping peacefully. It looked and felt like a perfect Spring day. On the way to Angie's house, I stopped at the corner store to spend the dollar my uncle had given me the day before. He gifted it to me as he had promised for me helping around his house. Back then, that offer meant a lot, as a dollar went a long way in those days. With a piece of candy costing a penny, a dollar meant a lot for me. I bought a dollar's worth of candy.

As I got to Angie's house, I heard her say "Girl, we're going to get in trouble if you get caught with all of that candy". But I had a plan to hide it in my bookbag before we got to the bus stop. If I didn't hide it, I would have gotten bullied for the whole bag. I managed to get through the day with no incidents. After school, Angie and I walked home. Angie's mother greeted us at the door, directing Angie to change out of her school clothes She invited her to go play tennis. She was a pro at it. The two of us were so excited as we ran into the room and jumped up and down on the bed. Just then, as the candy we had saved fell out of our pockets on onto the bed, her mother came in and said, "You both know better than that". She then said "Angie, we will take Jamillah home to ask her mother if she can come along".

I crossed my fingers as we got to the house. My mom peeked her head out the bedroom window as we knocked on the door. Just then, she yelled "Girl, stop knocking on the door so hard". She couldn't understand why I was so excited. She threw the key out of the window and I unlocked the front door. As I walked in, I told Angie to come with me to ask my mom if I could go with her. Angie agreed. She asked my mom if I could tag along, and my mother turned to me and asked "Jamillah, did you do your chores?" I was in charge of doing dishes. I gave her a blank stare as if her words were flying over my head. She looked at me and replied "Well, I guess you cannot go".

Angie looked at me confusingly and asked "Girl, you got chores at the age of nine?" I sorrowfully looked at her and my mother, realizing that I never get to go anywhere. My mom was so strict with us. We were only allowed to be in the sight of our siblings, right in front of the house, and outside until the streetlights came on. I begged Angie to ask her mother if she could ask my mother if I could go with them after I finished the dishes. I wanted her mom the patiently wait outside in their car with the windows down, in 75-degree weather, with the engine running, until I was done doing my chores.

Little did my mother know that Angie was downstairs helping me with the dishes in order for me to go. We were both at the sink on chairs, getting them done in less than ten minutes. I ran to the door after hearing a knock. Angie's mom got impatient. As I opened the door, her mom said "What's taking you two so long?". Angie blurted out "Mom, Jamillah has chores!" sarcastically rolling her eyes. She then asked her mom to ask my mother if I could tag along with them.

Angie's mom screamed from the bottom of the steps. "Mary, is it ok if Jamillah comes along with us to play tennis?". My mom replied, "Did she finish those dishes?" Her mother replied confirming they were done. I ran to my room and changed so fast and Angie and I ran out of the door quickly, fighting over the front seat. Angie's mother walked out the door and into the car, cranking her music up as we drove off listening to Soul Sonic Force's "Planet Rock". We started doing the wop to the beat of the music with all the windows down.

I just knew that her mother had to be the coolest mom on earth. We arrived at the tennis court and her mom took out all of her professional gear. She had all the professional gear and uniforms to match; short sleeved shirt, skirt, sun visor, sweatband and long socks. She was ready! We had a ball until the sun came down. As the sun went down, I said "Oh, it's time for me to go home". We packed everything up and as I headed up to the car, I looked at Angie and said "I wish I could stay the night at your house".

Only two of my brothers were with me at home, and this made it quite boring or at least I felt. Being the youngest made it that much worse. I was never able to stay out as late as the others. Angie looked at her mom when she dropped me off. Her mom answered her before she could even ask. "….the answer is no". We were both tired out. "See you tomorrow Angie" I said as I sadly returned to the house. I thanked her mom for letting me join them. I walked into the house where my mother was in the kitchen, cleaning after cooking.

She directed me to play with my younger brother Charles after dinner. She put my younger brother Tamir to sleep while Charles and I played with Playdoh in our room. We shared the second floor. Charles and I had a record player in our room. I was playing one of my mom's favorite songs; 'Reunited' by Peaches and Herb. After putting Tamir to bed, she came to our room and let us know she was getting in the tub. She gave me a directive shortly after. "If your dad comes, do not answer that door. Do you hear me?" My aunt Dot and her boyfriend Doc lived on the third floor with us at the time. They'd always play loud music, eating crab legs and shrimp every weekend.

While my mom was in the tub, she left the door cracked open a bit to enable her to hear just in case my younger brother woke up. I heard a loud knock on the door so I ran downstairs, thinking it might be my brother or sister. We had double doors and an entrance way to the front door. In order to see who was at the door, you had to open the first set of doors first. I had remembered my mom instructed me not to let my dad in, so I cracked the door slightly, noticing it was my father. I hadn't seen him in a while since my parents were experiencing a separation. I wasn't aware of the fact that she didn't want him to enter because their separation was due to him being unfaithful to her. I didn't remember too many bad times because she was secretive.

As I spoke to him, he pushed his way in and asked "Where is your mom?". The smell of liquor came out of his pores. I just knew I would be getting in trouble. He sat in the living room as my mother was getting dressed upstairs. I tried to apologize for letting him in. She looked at me like she was upset, telling me to go back into the room with my brother and to leave the door shut. It seemed unusual for her to have to tell me to so this. I immediately had a bad feeling. I turned the music down in our room just to hear their conversation. I heard my mom repeatedly ask my dad if he was drunk or high. My dad sounded upset at her repeated questioning.

I heard the kitchen drawer open as he went into the kitchen. My mom ran up the steps, screaming my aunt's name. Of course, she was unable to hear her, as her music was blasting as usual. I grabbed my brother Charles and held him because he was scared, covering his mouth so they wouldn't hear him crying. In my room, I couldn't get to my younger brother, who was sleeping in my mom's room on her bed.

I saw my mom run past our room first, heading to the third floor to alert my aunt that he was trying to hurt her. While she made her way to the third floor, she hid in my sister's room. My aunt eventually turned her music down as it appeared, she heard something. My dad had repeatedly been stabbing my mother, a total of THIRTY-TWO times, telling her to go to "Paradise". Coincidently, she had just turned 32. My Aunt, hearing the commotion, noticed my father running out of my sister's room with the lights off. She ran down to my mother's room to call the police. Her back was turned to us as she called the police and gave them the address, whispering information. As she whispered the information on the phone, my father had snuck up behind her and stabbed her repeatedly in her back. Her boyfriend heard her screaming his name and ran down the stairs. He looked in my mother's room and saw her bleeding all over the place. My dad was already halfway out of the door at this point with my aunt's boyfriend chasing him down.

By that time, I was knocking on all the neighbors' doors begging them to call the cops. My neighbor that lived on the corner house, an older couple, had offered my brother and I space to stay at her house. We cried ourselves to sleep that night. I jumped out of my sleep during the night, confused as we were sleeping on the floor surrounded by cats everywhere. For a second, I had forgotten what had happened. There was a knock on the door. It was my Aunt Vera looking for my brother and me. As we ran to her, she hugged me so tight and said "Baby, we believe in Jesus". I never understood what she was talking about back then.

She asked me to show the police where my mother was. ON our way home, I noticed my aunt on the stretcher in the ambulance with the paramedics giving her CPR. My aunt Pat grabbed me by the hand and said "Baby, show us where your mother is". I directed them to the third floor. Noticeably, all the lights on the third floor were out as we headed up the steps. My mother was lying by the side of the wall along my sister's bed. My aunt Pat turned the light on in my sister's room. You could see the blood splattered all over the wall, with my mom laying face upward on her back with her eyes wide open. My aunt Pat let out a loud scream, turning to me saying "Baby, please don't look". But it was too late. I looked anyway onto that horrible scene. It would be something that I could never forget.

Chapter Two
Now What?

We were leaving from aunt Vera's house. She lived around the corner from us. This day was the gloomiest day I had ever seen. The clouds looked dark, but no rain was coming down. You could hear nothing but the birds. The neighborhood was so quiet; it seemed as if the community was waiting for us to come outside just to see the look on our faces. I felt like we were being watched wherever we went all day. I honestly felt the empathy of Harrisburg. My mom was loved amongst many. My eyes were puffy from crying the past two days and I could barely keep them opened. It looked and felt like I had lost a fight. What are we going to do, I thought? Who is going to take care of us? Would we be in foster care or family?

I was in deep thought, reflecting on my nine years spent with my mom. The good and bad times made me smile but also hurt more to think about. I had a great relationship with my mother. She was kind, stern, humble, a hard worker with two jobs as a waitress and also a stenographer in the courthouse. She made our clothing, and also sponsored immigrant to stay in the U.S. She was what you call a Jack-of-all-trades.

On the day of the funeral, it felt like the paparazzi were following us. Winfield Funeral was so packed, it was as if people were standing outside of the funeral home for a celebrity's homegoing service. That is how well known my mother was. She was a dedicated hard worker. We got in closer to the casket. My mother looked beautiful, peacefully sleeping. It was one of the worst days of my life. I was told that the sheriff brought my dad to the funeral before anyone arrived. I guess it was due to him stating that he did not remember murdering my mother. The mayor was there to give his condolences. He was someone who kept up with me from childhood. After the burial, we all returned to my grandmother's house.

When we returned, there was a family meeting to decide which aunts would raise and take care of all of us. Aunt Dot was not fully recovered from being stabbed by my father. The family ultimately decided to separate us amongst the aunts. My aunt Betty took my younger brother Charles and I while Grams took my oldest sister and brother. There it was. We would all be divided but living in the same city. We knew we were in good hands, but things were not going to be the same anymore. We reflected on our Fridays when our mother would come home from work, excited to spend time with us. I would choose skating over the movies every time. I remembered her rules about having the house clean before we went anywhere. All four of us had chores that we had to do each day, and we knew her rule: "No work, no play". We got the floors so clean that you could eat off the floors. You could smell all the pine and incense doors down from our house when the screen door was open.

The neighborhood we lived in was peaceful, but busy with kids our age. I never wanted to leave Sylvan Terrance Street. The neighbors would not only look our each other, but we were also disciplined by our neighbors if our mom was at work. My older sister's responsibilities were to cook, clean, get us dressed and walk us to and from school. Our neighbors were Spanish so they would bring over Spanish rice and pork that smelled so good that you could smell it through the walls. Although we weren't allowed to eat pork, I would always be the one trying to jump across the banister when my parents weren't home and ask to try just a tiny piece. Before they got home.

When my dad came home, he would ask us what we learned for the day one at a time. My dad would ask "What did you learn today Fox?" whenever he got to me. I squeezed my lips tight so he could not smell pork on my breath, letting very little air out of my mouth as I answered " I had a good day at school dad". He'd ask "Why are you holding your lips so tight? I can smell pork on your breath". I'd shake my head and denied it, but my eyes told the whole truth. I knew I could not lie, that was my father's number one rule: Always be honest, no matter what the situation is".

As he looked at me he said "Open up your mouth wider and let me smell your breath". After smelling it, he said "Yes, I know it was you. Now go upstairs and keep your eyes on that picture of the hog". The hog was a poster sized picture my dad had on the third-floor wall as a punishment and reminder to not eat pork. It was a terrifying picture of a hog filled with rats, pigs, cows and animals that had pork in it coming out of the hog's mouth. When we were disobedient that was our punishment, and we weren't allowed to look away. We just stood there, with our legs and back hurting from standing, which was torture in its own way. That was a lesson learned not to eat pork and to never lie again.

In my mind I always thought" why would my mother allow this to happen?". Grandmom would disagree with mommy's choice of dealing with my dad's rules, but she would respect that he was her husband. My grandmother would tell me all the stories about my mom running away to be with my dad. She didn't care about the consequences she had to face as a teenager. She said my mom's "nose was wide open to that man". She followed his practice, not celebrating holidays, only birthdays. Grandmom finally had enough of that and would tell my mom to bring the kids up to her house to grab their gifts. We'd be so happy. She had a present for the whole block every Christmas and Easter. She would have us wrap them every summer. From then on, we had always looked forward to celebrating at grandmom's house. Her block was where all of the excitement was. She was everyone's grandmom Minnie.

Chapter Three
This Can't Be Happening!

Time passed by and My brother Charles and I were adapting to life with my Aunt Betty, getting to know our neighbors and kids our age. They asked a lot of questions about who my parents were and why I was living with my aunt. I figured my aunt would have already told them the story about my parents. After repeating the story time and time again, I begged them to not ask me again. It was too hurtful to even think about it. I still felt the void even after several years went by.

I was asked if I needed counseling at school, which I refused. High school was the worst time for me to discuss anything. I was more focused on getting to meet new friends in high school. I became well known and famous in high school, known as the shortest females at John Harris High School. I started dating at 15 yrs old. My boyfriend's parent held similar rules as my aunt Betty, not as strict as I would imagine. The freedom I had was because my aunt did not have trust issues when it came to me being involved with boy and I took advantage of that. I was well known for being short and for my character, the image that I held by keeping all of the hurt and bitterness inside.

One day in Journalism class a few classmates and I were cracking jokes on one another and laughing from the beginning of class until the end. Before class ended, two of my classmate friends started arguing, their jokes becoming serious. I remember it was a perfect Friday, and we all rode the bus to and from school. They were still arguing well into the bus ride home. The girl was so upset she told her boyfriend to meet her at the bus stop so he could address the boy who had now made jokes and bad words about her boyfriend. When we arrived to the bus stop her boyfriend was there waiting. As the crowd grew bigger, I felt his fear of not wanting to get off the bus. As a peacemaker and protector, I told him to get off the bus last, ensuring him that I'd make sure Mousey, the boyfriend, wouldn't hit him.

They were both my friends, and the thought of them fighting did not sit well with me. Mousey was good with his hands and everyone knew he could fight. I got in between the fight and told the other boy to run, he lived right by the bus stop. As soon as he had enough room to break, he started running and the crowd ran behind him. He made it into his house and his dad came outside with a shotgun asking who wanted trouble with his son. Everyone scattered.

Mousey and I had always taken the same route to walk home from the bus stop. This day, for whatever reason, we took a different route. As we walked down the street, I saw a car full of boys looking for trouble. I said, "Mousey look out, come this way". No sooner than we got close to Mousey grandmother's house than my classmate, the one who I'd help break free from Mousey, jumped out of his car with a gun. I heard one of his family members say, "Shoot him now!". My heart started jumping fast as if it would burst out of my chest. The young man pointed his gun, the same gun his dad pulled out, towards Mousey. I began to scream "Noooo! Run Mousey!" Inside I thought 'Why is this always happening to me?'

Cheers came from the people in the car as the young man's finger was on the trigger. He looked away as though he didn't want to shoot Mousey when the gunshots fired. He jumped back in the car and sped down the street so quickly, the car looked like it turned on two wheels. I looked and saw Mousey drop to the ground just staring at me. My nerves were so bad, and I begged Mousey to hold on. I said, "Hold on Mousey, I'm going to go tell your grandma". I repeated "Mousey, please hold on" as I ran as fast as I could to get to his grandma's house. I was so out of breath when I arrived that I couldn't get the words out to explain what was happening. I could only point to where Mousey was laying on the ground. We got to him and told the crowd around us to step back and call 911. I felt like they were taking too long to get here to help him. Everyone was surrounding him, and I kept saying "Please Mousey, just hold on, I hear them coming".

The paramedics arrived, ripping off his clothes to perform CPR. He opened his eyes, taking his last breath. I watched his chest move in and out for the last time. He rolled his eyes back, a light smile covering his face as he closed his eyes. Everyone started crying immediately. I was too scared to sleep for a while after that. My nightmares had returned.

Chapter Four
God, Please Make This Go Away!

After Mousey's death, I thought back to the second grade, and why I hated taking the school bus. It was close to the end of the school year and my childhood friend Aliyah and I were on the bus. Our bus driver was getting close to our drop off, stopping at Third and Kelker St. As we were getting off of the bus I got to the corner, looking both ways before I dashed across the street. Aliyah did the same but stopped briefly before her dash because her bookbag had dropped close to the tip of the bus. The driver didn't see her and dramatically ran her over. All of the parents on the scene started screaming and flagging the driver to stop the bus. Aliyah's little body laid under the bus, a horrible scene that was added onto the many I would never forget.

As the years went by more and more kids were getting hit by buses until they finally invented the stop sign control arm on the school buses for cars to stop so students could cross safely. I was raised in the Uptown area of Harrisburg. The neighbors looked out for each other and the kids in the neighborhood. That is how tight knit the neighborhood was at the time. There were dilapidated buildings that we sat in front of and hung out without fear of getting hurt. If someone knew our parents, they felt comfortable addressing us when we got out of line, were disrespectful or caught outside after the streetlights came on. If you came home and told on any of those adults disciplining you, you'd get another beating for telling.

When we returned to school, I remember the moment of silence held for Aliyah at the beginning of the school year. It took me a while to get adapted to riding the school bus again, and the loss of my friend made it difficult to make new friends, but eventually, I moved on. My first year of high school I was ready to meet new boys. That is when I started dating. I thought I was in love. My first love and I spent a lot of time together. My aunt Betty raised me to become independent by working and still maintaining a good grade average in school. Like most teens, I had responsibilities like cleaning and paying the phone bill since I was the one mostly using the phone. I would talk on the phone constantly until I fell asleep on it. I was talking on a three-way line and calling all my male friends. I conversed with many friends; I couldn't choose who I wanted to stop speaking to while I was in a puppy love relationship.

Eventually everything finally caught up to me while trying to juggle those boys around by playing on the phone. I was talking to my main boyfriend on the phone while I had another boyfriend on my front porch. Having multiple guy friends was fun until I started feeling bad. That day, I ran out of my back door to my girlfriend's house, asking her to help me choose which guy I should be with right now. That is the day I decided on Ronnie.

Ronnie, my brother and I would go swimming every day in the summer at the Uptown YMCA. One day, not too many people were swimming, so we stayed for about an hour playing 'Marco Polo'. I got tired and was ready to leave. An older guy who routinely sat around the bleachers in the swim area was there. He was known for being a pervert who watched girls go in and out of the pool and the shower room until he was left there alone as the females kept leaving due to being uncomfortable. When I got out of the pool, I felt that right eye of his staring down at me like a vulture which caused me to exit the pool quickly. I almost slipped towards the deep end close to the ladies' room. I turned the corner quickly, slipping and hitting my head in the shower room.

I was too afraid to look back and see who had seen me fall, and I was also nervous knowing the pervert was following me. I felt his presence near. As I was running to head in the bathroom stall, I rushed to put my clothes on, hiding my legs on the toilet seat so that he wouldn't see them. I shook nervously, wanting to scream at the same time for help. I watched his feet walking from stall to stall. As soon as I saw an opportunity to escape, I ran, but he caught up to me, grabbing my right arm. I back kicked him hard with all my might before he could get me on the ground. I dropped everything I had in my hand behind me. My shirt was ripped and all I could think about was this man raping me. I slipped away from him and began screaming at the top of my lungs so loudly that it scared him away. He ran in the opposite direction towards the men's shower room.

I ran to the staff room and let them know what had happened. He was gone, and there were no cameras in that area to play back. This man was already known for his perverted acts, and eventually ended up spending time in prison due to his repeated offenses and similar patterns with several other girls. I got outside as fast as I could and told Ron what had happened. "Boy, do you know what just happened to me?". Ron began to ran in the direction of the lockers, but I told him he had just missed him. Ron and I spent the rest of our time on the front porch.

Ron started hanging with the wrong set of people and doing things that were against his character. Eventually, he ended up in a juvenile detention center where he was sentenced to a few months. The summer was over, and it was time to head back to school. Ron would call me every day after school from the center at 3:30 PM. I would literally just be getting off from school. I knew to run straight home to receive the call. Months had passed by of him being at the center.

One day, as I was walking home from school, I decided to take a different route, a quicker one that I thought would get me home in time to receive Ron's phone call from placement. As I was speed walking home, my girlfriends saw me and stopped me on my way and asked, "Did you hear about Ron?" "My Ron?" I asked. The girl replied "Yes, your Ron". I replied, puzzled "No, was he cheating on me?". "No", she replied. "I heard on the radio that he was killed in a car accident". In disbelief I answered "Yea, right".

I ran home and turned the radio station to Wink 104. The first thing I heard was that there was a fatal accident on Interstate 83 and the young man's name was Ronald Tilman. "That can't be Ronnie" I said to myself. I had just spoken to him last night. I didn't take him seriously when he said he was going to escape from the detention center to come see me. I called his house and his younger brother answered the phone, crying on the other end. I heard his mother in the background crying. A hard knot formed in my throat as I began crying. "Is it true?" I asked his brother. "Yes, it's true". He replied. I put him on hold so he couldn't hear my screams. I shouted to my aunt that it was my boyfriend that had died. Several days went by, and my body had gone into a routine I'd come to know all too well. I couldn't eat nor sleep. After attending the funeral, I was lost. I slept on the floor in my aunt's room for several days because I had nightmares about him.

Chapter Five
I'm Not Built For This Anymore

I started staying to myself at this point, afraid to face another death. My aunt was cool, and she allowed my friends from the porch into the house. I had turned 16 and had the biggest sweet sixteen party on my block. I had flyers made and invited just about my entire high school. It was packed from the lower part of the house to the third floor, and spilled out into the Pharmacy parking lot across the street from the house. I felt grown, with so many people showing up from school and packing out the Rite Aid parking lot. I had my friend Ron Ski as the DJ, Harrisburg's best DJ who would later pass away from cancer.

I was in the 12th grade now., working two jobs and renting a room from an older guy whose wife left him for being strung out on drugs. He decided to allow me take over his property as long as I kept up with the utilities. I maintained all the bills, but the house was too much space for me. I decided to rent out rooms to keep up with the mortgage. I had it going on at this time. My bus stop was right on the corner so there was no excuse to be absent or late for school.

I began dating my partner in crime who was also my best friend's brother. We got into a lot of bad things together, from stealing cars to selling drugs, nickel and diming it, hustling enough money to keep up with the Jones'. Out of the short time that I did sell drugs, I was thankful to God I didn't get caught. I was barely home while attending high school, and during those years of school, I became a procrastinator and postponed everything I had going on in my life. I decided to move out of the house. I decided to move to a different area of town on the Hillside area, where all the main action as on Market Street.

Market Street was where most of the New York guys hung out. I was ready for fun. My best friend Cocey and I decided to share the same apartment on Market street, the main street on the Hillside.

I had to repeat the 12th grade, failing English by one point. Did I return to school for that one English class? Absolutely. I didn't care how I showed up to school, but I made it. Cocey and I started dating New York men who hustled right on Market St, a block away from our apartment. We took the hustle game from the street into our apartment. We barely got any sleep. My other girlfriend, who was also dating a New Yorker lived three blocks down. She would always give us a warning if the fed raided her apartment or if she heard any discussions about them hitting our house next.

One night, I warned everyone in the apartment that no drugs were allowed inside. It was time to clean house. We all were up that night, waiting for the drug task force to knock the door down. After 2AM, we figured they were not coming at all. We began blasting music, smoking weed and watching stand up comedy. Suddenly, I heard a ton of disturbing noises that sounded like something was being demolished. I asked Corey to turn down the music. I had heard something going on in the apartment beneath us. Just then I heard police screaming "Get on the ground now!" We looked at one another and said, "Here they come!" almost in unison. There were only two apartments on that building and we lived on the top floor. I knew that they were coming.

I turned the music and TV off and Cocey, our New York friends and I had stunned look on our face. We could hear the police running up the steps headed towards our place. They had a warrant of entry and barged the door down with guns drawn on us shouting "Harrisbug Police, get on the floor, everyone with your hands up!" They are not going to find anything, I thought to myself. We had cleaned up the house the day before. . The officers sent in a female officer and checked Cocey and I in our bathroom. I felt humiliated being searched everywhere. Our place was searched, leaving a mess all over the apartment. After they left, I cried myself to sleep.

The landlord found out and left an eviction notice on the door. We had 30 days to vacate. I called my friend Mel to let him know we needed funds to pay back what we owed the landlord for the damages to the apartment. I called Mel and spoke to him." Listen Mel, I'm seriously thinking about going to Job Corps and I really need to change my lifestyle." Mel's response was "How long will you need there? Which Job Corp are you going to?" I said "I'm going to Woodstock just outside of Maryland". I figured out the finances for the landlord and went to Job Corp.

I arrived at Woodstock looking for all the folks from Harrisburg. They knew we had to stick together like a prison gang. I called family and friends to let them know I had arrived safely but did not want to get used to staying the whole thirty days. After two weeks I was already homesick. I called my aunt and asked if she could call the main office and let them know I was homesick and ready to return home. I told her to promise I will go back to Job Corps after my first visit home. I could picture the look on my grandmom's face in disbelief. That didn't work.

The third week had passed by. My RA came down to my dorm room and says "London, we have an important call on the phone." I figured my phone call to my aunt worked. I started smiling form ear to ear as the RA and I walked towards the office. I grabbed the phone with excitement and said "Hey Grandmom". But it was Cocey. She asked, "When's the last time you spoke with Mel from New York?" I told her it had been just a week. And asked her why. She paused for a minute before speaking. "He was missing for three days, and they found him somewhere along some train tracks close to the woods". I started screaming. "Noooo Cocey, please don't tell me that, what happened to him?" She confirmed, saying that the only way they could even identify him was by a necklace he was wearing. True enough, it was Mel.

I could only remember him telling me he was in a confrontation with his baby's mother prior and they ended up in the hospital side by side. Cocey continued to explain that a couple of our crew were going to attend the funeral in New York to represent me. "Out of respect we are going to the funeral because we knew you loved Mel, also he was always there for us. I will also let all of them know you couldn't make the funeral' she concluded. I went back to my room and drenched my pillow up with tears. I told my RA and didn't attend any activities. I told my roommate Nikki, telling her I just need to go home. The following week

I went home. My crew gravitated towards me with their condolences, since they knew how close Mel and I were. Now, I am back in Harrisburg, grieving once again.

Chapter Six
The Shift

Headed back to my stomping grounds, I experienced the city this time living in a different area of Harrisburg: The South Side. The south was a bit more wild than Uptown, but I enjoyed hanging out there with my friend Nia. I was always welcome in any area of Harrisburg and had no enemies. I started hanging out with Nia and her boyfriend. She introduced me to his brother, and we started dating for several months. I got pregnant at the age of 20. I had little complications during my pregnancy. I had to take stress tests a few times. I was excited during my first pregnancy in knowing I was bearing a son. My son's father was at all my prenatal visits. He felt in order for the baby to be a full junior he would have to have his full name. We welcomed Anthony Lorenzo Ramsey Jr at 5lbs, 10oz.

He was tiny and handsome. After little Anthony was born, his father and I had differences and went our separate ways. He went away for two years and I would make sure he was able to continue being in his life no matter our circumstances. After Anthony turned 2 years old, I decided to go back to school to get my diploma from Cumberland Valley High School. I knew it was time to grow up and get my life in order this time because a child was involved. Cocey and I started working together. I would work various jobs to save for an apartment while staying with aunt Betty.

Cocey introduced me to her new boyfriend from New York, who introduced me to his cousin. I told Cocey that I was not in the mood to date anymore New Yorkers, being single now for two years. Cocey said "Girl, give it a try. I promise you he is the one for you. He is a laid-back kind of dude". I tried to play hard to get for a little while before giving in. As soon as we got together, I became pregnant. I ended up having a baby girl, DeA'sia Dockery, weighing 6lbs, 12oz. DeA'sia had her father's last name. She was so beautiful with a head full of hair. I told her father I did not want to be in anymore relationships. We held onto our relationship for the next seven years. In this time, I got pregnant again, and in my eight month of pregnancy we were married. We had another baby girl weighing 6lbs, 14oz. We named her Aveona Dockery. I said "This is it! I do not want any more kids. Three is a crowd". As I thought about it, I said "God, I get the message now!"

Chapter Seven
The Stronghold

"God, I know I asked to be married with children, but why am I going through so much with this man?" I had to sit and patiently wait for the signs to show themselves. I knew deep down in my heart he was a great person. I wasn't a saint myself when I got angry and upset with him, but I knew for sure I didn't deserve this. I suffered mental and physical abuse for years. I kept a lot from my family and friends, smiling on the outside but hurting badly on the inside because I didn't want to leave him.

Who was this really hurting? I thought to myself. Besides myself, it would hurt my children. I dragged them long enough through my journey of pain. We moved to VA. Anthony came home from his new school and said "Mom, they have the MS13 living out by this way". Confused, I asked him who that was. "A gang" he replied. Thoughts ran across my mind. Lord, I thought, please don't let him get attached to those folks.

Anthony had gotten comfortable with going to that school, surrounding himself around the ladies. They loved him. I noticed his grades started dropping, and I had thought it was because he was being Mr. Telephone man at night. I set up a conference with his teachers. They revealed that he was uncomfortable at school but didn't want to tell me because we struggled so much and moved around so much. I knew Anthony lacked needed attention from me. I recognized that my son was not only homesick but lacking the right attention from both of his parents. I told his teachers that I knew what to do with him, although I was too embarrassed to tell them of the marriage concerns. I agreed to keep a close eye on his actions. I thought I was strict enough of my kids.

Anthony ran into the house the next day from school, frightened. "Mom, those MS13 dudes just chased me from the bus stop". I asked why they were chasing him, of all individuals, not chasing someone else. He later explained that he was asked to join a gang and refused, so they beat him up. I had decided to move him back to Harrisburg for the summer, which I knew was what he wanted to hear. I was always running to keep my family in a safe environment. We ended up staying there for a year in VA before moving to MD. It felt like we were a military family with the constant transitioning.

 I made up my mind that I was going back to being involved in the church and do right with God. I took the kids along, even if they complained from time to time. Overall, they enjoyed the services. I finally allowed Anthony to go to Harrisburg that summer. However, he ended up in some trouble up there, so I wasn't sure if he was the leader or the follower. I was so upset with him. He was on probation and had community service hours for his actions. His probation officer asked me what I thought would best fit for Anthony's actions. I asked about his options. His probation officer mentioned boot camp, and that rang a bell in my head. "Yes! That would work perfectly for him" I said. I felt he needed that good male structure that he wasn't receiving at home. IT was hard for me as a single mother to provide him the needed attention and turn a boy into a man.

 I referred to him as the 'man of the house' which ended up being a mistake. I thought teaching him responsibilities was great, but the title lead him to feelings of rushing him into his manhood prematurely. He wasn't able to be a kid and grow at his own pace. He did six months at boot camp. We kept in touch through letters and weekend phone calls. He begged me to move back to Harrisburg because he missed his friends. With everything I was going through, I did just that, and moved back to Harrisburg. Anthony was so excited. I threw a surprise party when he returned home from camp. I did not understand why every time I passed the highway sign that read "Welcome to Pennsylvania" I would get anxiety. Was it a sign I wasn't supposed to return home?

Chapter Eight
A Time for Change

I was attending Empire Beauty School and ultimately became a certified Hair Beautician. A few days before graduation, my instructor came up to me and said "Ms. London, you have an important phone call from your sister Jackie". A familiar knot began to form in my throat. I took a deep breath in and in my mind, I wondered who it could be about this time. "Lord, please not my grand mom, I just talked to her all night on the phone" I pleaded silently. We had talked about my plans to move to VA for a change of life for my family and I. "Hello Jackie" I said into the phone. Jackie responded quickly. "Yes Jamillah, you need to get here to the hospital. It's Grandmom". I rushed out of class, driving fast and disregarding stop lights and stop signs to get to the hospital. When I arrived, my grandmother was plugged up to several machines, tubes, and IVs, unresponsive. "God, we just lost grandpop a couple years ago we need grandmom" I thought. This family will fall apart without her. She was the main warrior holding the family together.

The family gathered around her praying and watching her suffer for two weeks. When the doctor told the family to meet him in the conference room, we knew to expect bad news. Her kidneys had begun to fail. I left the conference room and went back to say my last goodbyes to my grandmother. I prayed first, then told her I would continue my goals and plans we had discussed. I spoke to her gently."Grandmom, remember I told you I'm going to move to VA? You told me before I decided to relocate to think about it first before going and being disappointed? Well, I gave it some deep thought, and I can't live here without me if you leave me. So please, be strong and fight grandmom. We need you".

The doctor came in and said that the family had agreed to pull the plug. She had been suffering so long and only had two weeks to stay on life support. I was so upset because Grandmom and I talked about this to my uncle John, her only son, when he was on life support. I was so upset because I had hoped and believed that God would heal her. Miracle can happen. But it was too late. We all met on the third floor of the hospital to say goodbye to our grandmother. A flashback came to me, remembering how grandmom would say 'Miracles happen if we all pray'. I decided to have a little more faith and go in the room alone and pray with grandmom. I watched a tear fall from her closed eyes. I knew she heard my voice. I whispered to her to open her eyes or squeeze my hand if she heard me. A tear rolled down her face. I called the doctor in the room, yelling "My grandmother is responding". The doctors tried to resuscitate her, but it was too much on her heart. She no longer had to suffer from Emphysema. That very same day, my youngest daughter Aveona got very sick out of nowhere and was hospitalized form that day until the day of my grandmother's funeral. She was not able to walk or talk. Doctors did not know what was going on with her.

Things were happening left and right. I heard that someone stole our car, crashed it and left it smashed up Uptown. I said "Lord, please, help me because I can't take anymore". Two years later, I relocated to VA, believing things would change and get better. Moving to a state where I knew no one but my girlfriend. I loved the atmosphere, the air and the possibility to do more in VA. The kids loved it there. My son was always the type of kid who could adapt well with others quickly. He had friends within 2 weeks. The girls, however, were shy. I started working doing the same type of work I did in Harrisburg. I was making more money due to cost of living and would often invite friends and family down to my house after a few months.

On one occasion I had invited them down to party and we went out and partied until 4 AM, even though I had to be at work by 6 AM. We had a great time until we returned to my house and an argument with my husband and I took place in front of them. I had to call off of work and the kids saw and heard everything. I was embarrassed that my family had finally witnessed the abuse I had been hiding for years. After the fight, my family left for Harrisburg. It was just the kids and I that remained for a little while. As I sat one day I thought, my grandmother was right. Although she loved my husband, I had made a promise that I was not moving back to Harrisburg.

Chapter Nine
Anthony

Moving back home to Harrisburg felt like a curse from hell. Things were going great at first. Anthony got his license and started working a full-time job. I brag about him achieving both. His job was temporary, but I was happy that he was able to get his first car. It took a lot of weight off of me and he was able to help me out and pick the girls up from school. When his job ended, he was a little frustrated. He always wanted to see me holding on strong to my independence. Anthony was discouraged about not finding another job and started hanging out with his friends on the Hillside area. I started worrying about him more.

"What is going on over there on the hill that is causing you to stay out so late?" I asked. He explained how faithful and loyal he was to his friends. One day Anthony came into my room out of breath. "Mom, you won't believe what just happened to me". I asked him to catch his breath before trying to talk. He explained New Yorkers approached his friend and stated they needed to get off the block before something happened. He continued saying everyone scattered but him, and they eventually ended up in a shootout, and one of the bullets put a hole in his sneaker. Showing me the sneaker, I replied "Boy, you better get on your knees right now and thank the Lord that you are alive". I got on my knees, immediately starting praying, thanking God for saving my son.

A couple of weeks went by and I noticed Anthony hanging with the same New York group of friends. They had taken them under his wing. I knew they must have had some strong hold on him. They were older and using him to cover up for what they were doing. They figured he was the perfect young man because he had heart. One day, I picked him up from Vernon street and on the way home, I spoke to him about the plans I had for him to move to Charlotte, NC and join the military, just to get him to move away from the city and returned as a changed man with my nephew.

During the discussion, Anthony changed the subject and stated he noticed I had lost weight. "Yes" I said, "from worrying about you out here in these streets." He replied "Mom, I'm not doing anything out here but chilling with the homies". When we got to the house, I could hear the Spirit say "I'm preparing you" I had no idea what that meant. I felt weird even hearing that but took heed to it. It was a beautiful day outside; birds were chirping close to the window. I did my usual Saturday morning cleaning with fresh Pine-Sol and bleach. My friend suggested I should have a cookout that day and invite family and friends. I did just that.

We played all the old school games like 'red light, green light', relay races, and more. Anthony was getting dressed and entered the kitchen to ask me how he looked. "You look nice" I replied. He started bopping to the music and dancing with his cousins. He was smiling from ear to ear. Someone called his phone and said they were out front to pick him up. Usually, I check to see who comes for him, but for some reason that day I hadn't. I was busy entertaining my company. As Anthony left, he yelled "Mom, I'll be right back" over the music. I nodded to him. He repeated himself "I promise mom, I'll be right back'.

By 9PM, I shut the cookout down and went to sleep. Anthony did not call nor come back home. I got up, went to work and physical therapy. While at the sauna at therapy, I was chatting with a church member from my old church. Feeling a weird feeling overcome me, I asked if she could pray for me. She asked what the prayer request was. I told her I didn't know, but that I just needed prayer. As I drove home afterwards, I told my daughter to go play with her friends around the corner. I came through the backdoor into my house. As I put the key in the door, I noticed two detectives. They approached me and asked me if I resided at this address. I replied that I did. They asked if I knew who Anthony Ramsey was and my relationship to him. "He is my son" I said. "what did he do?" They looked at each other and swallowed hard. I said "Well, what did he do?". One officer began to reply." Well Ma'am, Anthony was shot last night" I interjected "Where? On his body?". They gave each other that look as if trying to decide who would deliver the bad news. The detective asked if anyone was home with me. "Is he ok?" I asked. The detective replied "No, he was killed in Middletown, PA last night around 9:34PM". I let our a loud scream at the top of my lungs;"They killed Anf". I hadn't realized I had my brother on speed dial and he lived down the street from me. I immediately remembered and he was at his job, right around the corner. I couldn't get my words out quick enough. I just kept repeating myself saying "They killed Anf".

My frustration turned to the detectives. "How and why are you contacting me sixteen hours later is Anf had his license with our current address on it". My brother got to my house in what seemed like less than 5 minutes from when the detectives had delivered the news. I didn't trust them at all. I had the weirdest feeling that they were withholding information. Because I was in shock, I ran to the third floor to his room to make sure I wasn't being pranked. I called his phone repeatedly waiting to hear his voice on the other end. I sat in his room so long that when I came down, my house was packed. I got on the phone with detectives from Middletown, PA and asked, "what happened to my son". He responded with "Ma'am the reason why we are not answering you is because we don't want to talk to you" Confused, I probed further "Why, what did you do to my son?" He replied saying they would rule it as a justifiable homicide with not enough evidence.

They explained a gun was involved that Anthony had pulled out on the murderer's sister and he told her he was giving her five seconds to bring money out of her pockets. The informant, they explained, pulls out a gun and shot Anthony four times in his upper body and 1 bullet in his back. They did not give me any information on who killed my son until a year later. I reached out to our State Rep, asking for help with my son's case. We went to the DA for questioning as he ruled it self-defense, only to find that my son's fingerprints were not found on the gun he was accused of having. I asked several of his friends that were with him that day if Anf had a gun before he got in the car with the men from New York. They all provided the same story that he did not. This left my son's murder with no clear answers or justice. What had happened to my son, and who set him up to be murdered?

I moved out of my house after Anthony's death. I could no longer live there with all the precious memories that haunted me every day. Not only seeing his spirit but feeling his presence in the house all day. I prayed and asked GOD to allow his spirit to connect with me and reveal what had happened to him. I was so devastated at what was revealed. It was like a huge puzzle trying to place all the pieces together. After being in the new place for a year, my oldest daughter gave birth to my first granddaughter. It was two weeks before Christmas. We were getting ready to take the baby to her first doctor's appointment when I advised my daughter to heat the car up for the baby.

I turned on the car engine, but noticing they weren't ready, I turned off the engine to the car, leaving my purse inside since it was in the carport. I returned back to the house and heard the alarm. We heard a loud BOOM. We ducked nervously thinking someone outside was shooting. I told my daughter to stay in the living room while I checked to see what was happening. Once I opened the back door, smoke started to fill the house. I told my daughter to gran my granddaughter and her sisters and go out the front door. I began to knock on the neighbor's house informing them of the fire. The flames began to spread into the back of my house. My daughter began to scream and ran down the street. The fire Department arrived after a while, stating they could not find the house. I felt like the entire neighborhood would have gone up in flames.

I am thankful GOD did not allow us to get into the car at that moment, drive off and blow us up. I suppose the car had an engine malfunction, although the mechanics just did work on the car. I was already paranoid life after my son Anthony was murdered. Thank God the enemies' plan did not work.

Chapter Ten
The Secret Storm

Anthony Lorenzo Jr was murdered in Middletown, PA on West Main St. in an apartment building. The suspense was that there was an assailant that took him to Middletown, drove the vehicle to the building, and had texted the murderer that they were sending Anthony into the building. After my son's unexpected death, I said to myself "I am not going to sit around in silence and let my son's blood be on these people's hands, including some officials". Every time I went to the DA's office to seek answers, their responses never changed.

They explained that they were ruling my son's death as self defense without evidence and justifiable homicide. If the DA had more facts and evidence to prove Anthony was guilty of this criminal offense, I could shake it off and say Anthony was wrong for his actions. I am a mother that never justified what her son might have gotten himself into while away from home. Several others, including myself, felt strongly that my son was set up to be murdered by a murderer. His case was closed right after his death. Murder cases can be reopened after a few years. I am still seeking answers. I did a follow up to reopen his case and have still received no answers. My fight is not over.

I want to encourage mothers to know that even though we raise our children to the best of our knowledge and capabilities, our children are assigned from God. Proverbs 2:6 states we should "Raise up a child in the way that they should go, and they will not depart from it". Ephesians 6:4 says "Fathers, do not exasperate your children; instead, bring them up in training and instruction of the Lord"

I was watching the Michael Brown trial after seeing across the screen something that read "Self Defense or Murder?". I began to light candles by Anthony's picture., preparing breakfast and cleaning. I walked out of the kitchen feeling lightheaded and dizzy. I remembered hitting the floor later to wake up and see my significant other on top of me performing CPR with tears in his eyes. He rushed me to the hospital. I could hear the doctors telling him he had brought me right on time. I had a seizure for the first time in my life due to high amounts of stress, leaving three white spots on my brain. Doctors couldn't determine whether it was from Lupus which I was diagnosed with, a stroke or MS. I was just happy to be alive. I realized that losing a child caused me to enter a health storm. God sent his angel right on time for me. Stress will kill you if you allow it to overtake you.

Here are some words of encouragement. Please take care of yourself. Losing a loved one can be a lifetime of pain but know that you are left here to carry on a purpose. Thank God for Michael Burton, an angel sent here, for allowing God to help him to save my life.

As an exercise, take time to jot down some notes in a journal. Focus on the following questions. Your pain might not be like mine, but we can all be blessed by someone's story.

1. How can you begin to comprehend the bad news after a loss?
2. Did you feel numb after the first few days of losing your loved ones?
3. Did grief change your relationship with God?
4. Did drugs and alcohol play a role in coping with your pain?
5. Did you blame yourself for your loved one's death?

If you are ever in need of someone to talk to or if you have questions on learning how to cope with the loss of a loved one, please feel free to email ladyjamillah45@gmail.com. For more information about the murder of my son, please watch the documentary on You Tube entitled "Just One Victim's Families Speaks Out".

2nd Edition Notes: Handling the Storm

Chapter 2:

Dealing with PTSD after the death of my mother brought flashbacks, memories, nightmares and scary thoughts repeatedly to my mind. I was trying to handle the situation by myself, refusing the counseling being provided to me. I know now that I should have taken advantage of that. Especially not knowing then that so much more tragedy would hit me. Counseling would have been the best thing that would have helped me to cope positively during those hard times. Share how you're feeling during times of difficulties. Leaving it pent up inside of you can lead to other issues down the line. Share with someone who might relate, or who has experienced something similar. Cognitive Behavior Therapy is an effective tool for people who develop PTSD. Seeking support from loved ones helps as well.

Chapter 3:

Witnessing a murder once again was devastating for me. This one was a unique experience. I was friends with both the person who committed the murder and also with the victim. I constantly played in my mind the tragedy from both very different angles. I found it hard to sleep again. I was plagued with nightmares prior to that happening which caused a lack of rest and low scores and GPA. I did not know what life was like without fear and death constantly around me. In this chapter, I had to navigate grief with living a day to day life and keeping things in order by any means necessary in order to survive after experiencing so much death. This chapter was important for me because it taught me to understand how to navigate so many feelings from many different perspectives, as the person who lost, knowing a murderer and experiencing sympathy for the victim.

Chapter 4:

I thought life would be easier by looking for love in order to replace this feeling of loss and loneliness. I was desperate to bring my mind back from feelings of void and bring it back to where it needed to be, which was that peace and understanding that I couldn't find after loss. I started dating, spending time with my boyfriend in order to share laughter, love and good and bad experiences with someone. To hear how much he wanted to spend time with me during his experience was crushing, adding only to it the devastation I felt when he ended up losing his life in a tragic car accident to get to me. This made me feel like I could no longer live on. Although grief is a natural part of life, at this point I couldn't help to think: How much more could I actually take? Times like this of devastation are normal when tragedy happens so close together. I was not soon healing from my previous tragedy when another one crept up on me and knocked me right back down.

Chapter 5:

Trying to suppress the pain by partying, having my own apartment and selling drugs were all a part of how I chose to deal with grief. Keeping up with school but being unfocused on my career got me nowhere. In meeting new faces, I developed lots of friendships to fill the void, but they only ended up being more bad influences and putting me deeper into a lifestyle that ended in tragedy. The fact that someone I cared for had died and I was in Job Corp unable to attend his funeral impacted me. Forming close relationships and losing someone without being able to say goodbye creates bigger levels of depression.

Chapter 6:

When life beats you up, what more can you do but change your situation? When feeling like a failure and cursed with death all around you, you may not think there is anything you can do to get out of the curse. Taking self inventory lead me to make a change. I was afraid to meet death. I decided to make the needed changes for my first born son.

Giving birth and becoming a mother added a second layer of purpose and it helped me combat feelings of death with feelings of new life.

Chapter 7 &8:
Finding a man who wanted to be married the way I wanted to be was one of the best choices in life that I thought I had made. Later, it ended up being nothing that I ever wanted to experience. I ended up with more beautiful girls but was living in a nightmare. Without counseling in a marriage, it can feel like you are sleeping with a stranger with no clear direction on how to move forward. I ended up paying the price for the title of being someone's wife. Eighteen years of bad outweighing the good. Mental and physical abuse took place in silence. The lesson or me was learning that our children should never have to suffer through our mistakes and choices that we decide to make. These choices might feel like they are done with them in mind, but they end up causing more stress to them and they can become rebellious, disobedient, and violent as a result of what they see, hear, and experience.

Chapter 9:
Coping with losing my son felt nearly impossible. There will never come any day, minute, second, nor hour that I will stop thinking of my son. When I speak his name, it might make others uncomfortable, but not for me. His life mattered to me. Grieving is for a lifetime. Let no one tell you the solution is to 'get over it'. No one can fix our broken hearts. This club of grieving mothers is not one I ever expected to have full membership in and it is a club I never wish for anyone else to join. However, through processing his death, I realize it is a club that I never want to avoid. I find peace in encouraging other mothers. I encourage every mother who has lost a child to hold dearly to the memories shared. Whether it is birthdays, holidays, or even memorial anniversary days, those days are all impactful at keeping a person's memories alive. Memorial anniversaries are very hard for me. They feel like torture, but they also help to remind others that your child is still with you in spirit.